NATURE'S FRIEND

THE
❧ GWEN FROSTIC ❧
STORY

WRITTEN BY

LINDSEY McDIVITT & EILEEN RYAN EWEN

ILLUSTRATED BY

PUBLISHED *by* SLEEPING BEAR PRESS

Gwen followed her brothers and sisters everywhere, like a small fawn follows its herd. They roamed the woods and fields near Croswell—their tiny town tucked into the thumb of Michigan. Gwen played and picked wildflowers. But her hands were weakened from an illness as a baby. Her speech was slurred, one small foot dragged, and she fell down often.

She bumped her shins.

She bruised her knees.

She banged her elbows.

"Gwen doesn't need your help, Helen," Mama called from the porch. Mama knew Gwen could do whatever she put her mind to.

"I never knew I couldn't do something."
—Gwen Frostic

Gwen was born in 1906 and at that time, a child with disabilities usually stayed home. But Mama had been a teacher—she sent Gwen to school and pushed her to learn.

In class, Gwen hated the glances and giggles. She hated the whispers. And, most of all, she hated that the only things other students seemed to notice were the things that made her different. It made her want to hide like a frightened chipmunk. But instead, Gwen gathered up knowledge like a bird builds a nest.

Gwen was bright, but her hands were weak. Her teachers said she would never learn to write. Mama stuffed a drawer with art supplies and encouraged Gwen to use her hands. Gwen pulled out a pencil and pad of paper. Like a new leaf stretching for the sun, she reached for new skills.

Her hands worked extra hard. She sketched and scribbled. She doodled and drew. Gwen's grip grew stronger and stronger.

Gwen loved learning, but trying to make friends could leave her feeling as prickly as a porcupine. Nature felt like a friend, pulling her out to play. With so much to discover, Gwen didn't have time to feel lonely.

Swaying grasses whispered in fields thick with Queen Anne's lace.

Tiny ferns unfurled at her feet.

Frogs lapped up bugs with long, quick tongues.

Gwen breathed it all in. She listened to their message.

"all things are vital to the universe...
all are equal...and at once...different."

–Gwen Frostic, *Beyond Time*

When Gwen was 12, her family moved to the edge of Detroit. They rode the streetcar into the big city and gazed up at the Woolworth and Ford buildings. Long walks to Grosse Ile brought Gwen close to the nature she loved so dearly.

She was learning it was all right to be different, and high school brought new challenges. However, Gwen knew she could do anything she put her mind to and her hands, now strong and sure, reached for paintbrushes and paint.

She was unafraid to tackle tools and skills reserved for boys. Gwen signed up for mechanical drawing—learning to use rulers and compasses to draw machines—and the men squawked like angry blue jays.

But in shop class, her skills with a band saw impressed her classmates. *Bzzzz.*

In art school, Gwen discovered something new—linoleum, a rubbery material used for floors. Gwen grasped a sharp tool and worked hard to cut out a picture in the surface of the linoleum, carving it slowly and carefully. She rolled ink along the surface of the block and then gently pressed a clean sheet of paper to it.

"Her brush, her pencil and her pen will make this world a better place!"
—In Gwen's high school yearbook

Gwen dreamed of life as an artist. But in order to earn enough money to live, she knew she would need to start a business—though that wasn't easy for a woman back then.

One day, squaring her small shoulders, Gwen hopped on a bus to collect new art materials. She hauled home heavy loads of copper and brass.

Pounding away in Mama's basement, she hammered the metal into clocks, a sundial, and a fireplace screen decorated with dragons. The banging and clanging bounced off the cellar walls.

At first only Gwen's family cheered her creations, but word of her art was spreading across Detroit like a wildfire. Clara Ford, wife of automaker Henry Ford, ordered Gwen's copper vases for Fair Lane, their grand estate. In 1939, Gwen was invited to send her art to the World's Fair in New York. She felt like a bird on the first day of spring.

Soon war broke out in Europe and the copper and brass Gwen loved to use disappeared—all metal went to manufacturing equipment for the armies overseas. She wanted to lend a hand.

Gwen knew she could do whatever she put her mind to. She marched into the Ford Motor Company and signed up to build bombers. Ford's famous assembly line now produced a plane every hour. Using the mechanical drawing skills she had learned, Gwen designed tools for building the airplanes that were desperately needed for fighting in the war far away.

"All the day long, whether rain or shine,
She's a part of the assembly line.
She's making history, working for victory,
Rosie, brrrrrrrrr, the Riveter."
—Lyrics to "Rosie the Riveter" by Redd Evans & John Jacob Loeb (1943)

Gwen's days were filled with the roar of machinery and the clang of construction. But in the quiet evenings she still longed to create art. She reached again for linoleum. She bought a printing press and launched Presscraft Papers stationery company.

   Clickety CLACK,
     clickety CLACK,
       clickety CLACK.
   Gwen joined the small ranks of female business owners.

  But something was missing from Gwen's city life, and nature called to her like a friend. She pictured the wild north she loved so much— windblown trees, crashing waves, a great blue heron perched at the edge of a pond.

  She packed up her press and moved with her dog, Teddy, to the top of Michigan's mitten.

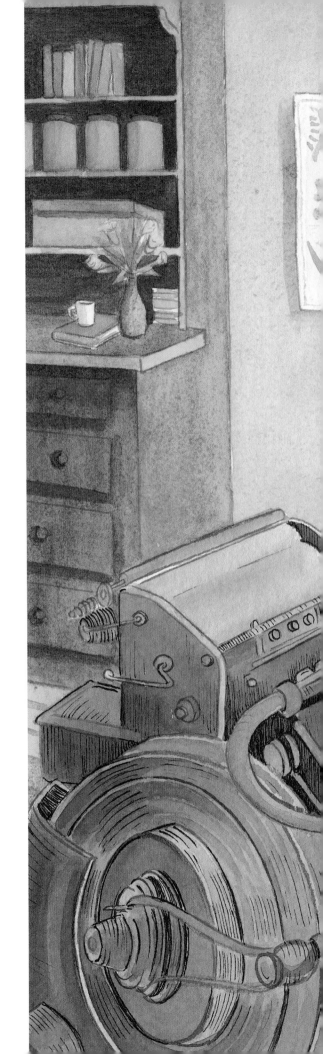

On her way to Lake Michigan's Betsie Bay, Gwen walked through Frankfort's tiny downtown. Her new neighbors definitely noticed Gwen and her dirty hands and ink-stained dress. They wondered why she and Teddy lingered so long at the swamp.

"I work with nature
because it treats me equally."
—Gwen Frostic

She walked deep into the wetlands.
When Gwen sat quietly with her pad and pencil,
as still as a watchful fox:
She seemed to hear music.
She sensed magic.
She witnessed small miracles.

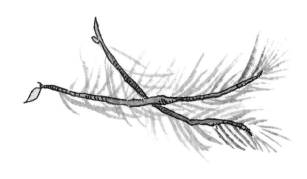

Gwen wanted others to see nature as she did, to recognize the value of plants, trees, and animals.

So she chipped and chiseled and cut—carving linoleum away until her designs stood out:

Graceful branches bare of leaves reached for the sky.

A lonely doe gazed over a grove of pines.

Whiskers twitched below a mischievous black mask.

Her linoleum blocks were ready for printing. Gwen ran them through her presses, and soon her new greeting cards were ready to sell.

"I do a pencil sketch from life—animals, birds, plants—trace it on the block and excise it for the press. Every vein in every leaf is true to life."

—Gwen Frostic

Gwen's art reminded everyone of nature's beauty and importance at a time when many people had forgotten. Lakes, plants, and animals were in trouble—threatened by pollution.

But like a fresh breeze through the birch trees, Gwen's work whispered truths about meadows and marshes. Across Michigan and around the world, people listened. Visitors flocked to her shop in the forest.

For many years, Gwen worked hard in her studio, surrounded by the woods and wetlands she loved. She was determined to show others that nature was worth protecting and enjoying. So much depended on it, and Gwen knew she could do whatever she put her mind to. Like ripples on the pond, Gwen's art spread the word—

"Love this earth,

    Love its waters...

        Care enough to keep it clear."

Gwen Frostic

"As long as there are trees in tiny seeds...there will be miracles on earth."
—GWEN FROSTIC, *A WALK WITH ME*

More about Gwen Frostic

As a pioneering woman in art and business, many times Gwen Frostic forged ahead when others were certain she'd fail. In 1964, she moved Presscraft Papers from Frankfort to 40 acres on the Betsie River, not far from Lake Michigan. Many feared for her business, but the fairylike shop in the forest thrived. Crowds drove dirt roads to the magical spot and mail orders arrived from around the world.

Gwen Frostic's greeting cards and books celebrated Michigan plants and wildlife. She wrote and illustrated 22 books and gave presentations all over Michigan, charging nothing. Gwen believed people would protect only what they noticed and appreciated. She was one of many trailblazers who raised the profile of the new environmental movement.

Gwen's work was widely admired, and Michigan heaped accolades upon her, including honorary degrees from five Michigan universities and awards from the Girl Scouts, garden groups, the Michigan Audubon Society, and the National Wildlife Federation. May 23rd was proclaimed Gwen Frostic Day by the governor in 1978. Gwen was inducted into the Michigan Women's Hall of Fame in 1986.

Late in her life, Gwen donated 13 million dollars to her alma mater, Western Michigan University in Kalamazoo—money earned from her own hard work. The university renamed its art school the Gwen Frostic School of Art. Her generous donation funds facilities, awards, and scholarships in art, creative writing, and environmental studies.

Gwen refused to be told what she could and could not do. She lived with physical challenges, yet she never saw herself as disabled. Gwen challenged society's expectations of people with disabilities and women in that era. As she grew older, she bucked the belief that older adults have no new ideas. Gwen worked in her shop until just a few years before her death in 2001, one day before her 95th birthday.

Happily, Gwen Frostic's legacy lives on. Her shop

remains open—looking much as she left it, from the stone foundation and grass-covered roof to the animal footprints that scurry across the floor and the small spring-fed fountain in the corner. Her Heidelberg printing presses still print cards from the same linoleum blocks carved by her hardworking hands. Visit! And help spread the word of nature's importance. Gwen would like that.

—Lindsey McDivitt

Sketch or Print with Nature

MATERIALS:

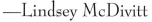

* Paper (keep some extra as scratch paper)
* Sharp pencils, eraser, and sketchbook
* Paints
* Newspaper or plastic to protect your table from paints
* Thin gloves to protect hands from paints
* Small paint roller and palette OR a paintbrush and cup

1. Find a favorite spot in nature and sit quietly as Gwen Frostic would. Observe the plants, trees, birds, and other creatures that live there.
2. Look for flowers, leaves, grasses, and bits of bark you find interesting.
3. Try sketching what you see. Notice tiny details and have fun drawing what you observe.
4. For printing, collect interesting flowers, leaves, or bark—but only with permission. Be considerate with nature. Never take bark or branches off a tree. Remove only a small part of any plant and leave roots in the ground so the plant can keep growing.
5. In your work space, put paint in your palette or cup.
6. Pick your first item and place onto scratch paper. Paint lightly over the entire surface to the edges.
7. Lift carefully and place paint side down on a fresh piece of paper. Press it down gently and try not to let it move.
8. Gently pull the item up and observe your nature print!
9. Print with different items or different colors. Make notecards or books like Gwen Frostic did!

For my children.
And for those who see, and protect our natural world, for *their* children.
—Lindsey

✣

For Stephen, with Love
—Eileen

Photo credits:
© Alan R. Kamuda/Detroit Free Press via ZUMA Wire
© Virginia Jones/My Knapsack on My Back
© Western Michigan University

Text Copyright © 2018 Lindsey McDivitt
Illustration Copyright © 2018 Eileen Ryan Ewen
Design Copyright © 2018 Sleeping Bear Press

Sleeping Bear Press™
2395 South Huron Parkway, Suite 200, Ann Arbor, MI 48104
www.sleepingbearpress.com
© Sleeping Bear Press

Printed and bound in the United States.
10 9 8 7 6 5 4
Library of Congress Cataloging-in-Publication Data
Names: McDivitt, Lindsey, 1957- author. | Ewen, Eileen Ryan, illustrator.
Title: Nature's friend: the Gwen Frostic story / written by Lindsey McDivitt; illustrated by Eileen Ryan Ewen.
Description: Gwen Frostic sought solace in art and nature. She learned to be persistent and independent--
never taking no for an answer or letting her disabilities define her. An artist and business owner,
Gwen dedicated her work and her life to reminding people of the wonder and beauty in nature.
Ann Arbor, MI : Sleeping Bear Press, 2018. Audience: Ages 6-10. Identifiers: LCCN 2018014169 | ISBN 9781585364053
Subjects: LCSH: Frostic, Gwen--Juvenile literature. | Artists withdisabilities--United States--Biography. | Artists as naturalists--United States.
Classification: LCC NX512.F76 M39 2018 | DDC 811/.54 [B] --dc23 | LC record available at https://lccn.loc.gov/2018014169